What Papa Told Me

By Felice Cohen

What Papa Told Me

ISBN (978-0-615-37288-4)

www.whatpapatoldme.com

Dividends Press

Cover design by www.maggiecousins.com

Printed in the United States of America
First Edition

For Papa

Thank you for never giving up

"Everyday's a birthday when I get up in the morning."
-- Murray Schwartzbaum,
August 15, 2006

"When I die, make sure I shouldn't be buried alive."
-- Murray Schwartzbaum,
July 11, 2007

Foreword

"*Feigela*," Papa's eyes were moist as he spoke my Yiddish name. "I want you should write my story." He was looking out a glassed-in porch, four stories above a deeply green manicured lawn where a serene blue river cut precise S-shapes throughout. Animating this Disney-perfect shoreline were dozens of bright white herons, while common hawks flew overhead. We were sitting on the terrace in one of several identical condominiums inside Papa's gated community in Boca Raton, Florida.

"But it's not just in the camps I had to survive," Papa said. "All my life I've come up against roadblocks and had to find ways to push through. I lived my life always with my kids in mind. I want they should know my story so that they can learn to survive, too."

Ever since I started writing for my college newspaper Papa had thought of me as "The Writer." That's why he wanted me to write about the personal struggles he faced in childhood, in the Holocaust, and then when he came to America. He had never told anyone these stories before. Not to his first wife nor his second current wife, nor to any of his five children, nine grandchildren or ten great-grandchildren.

"People should know," Papa had decided, "so that it doesn't happen again. I lost most of my family - parents, sisters, a brother, cousins, so many killed. I suffered conditions you shouldn't know from. But I never complained. I'm just an ordinary man who lived his life."

I took out a notebook.

Here is what Papa told me.

Felice: *Do you ever have nightmares of those days?*

Papa: *Sometimes, but I try not to think about it. There are some mornings when I wake up and feel like I'm suffocating and I have to run out and take a deep breath. (Pauses) I want you should put all these stories of the concentration camps together, one after the other, how I survived.*

Felice: *Okay, Papa. I will.*

1

In the Beginning

My name is Murray Schwartzbaum. I had a regular, normal childhood. At least it started off normal. I had the usual: a mother and father, one older brother, and four sisters. We all lived together, along with my grandmother, in a small house that had an extra room with a separate entrance that my parents rented to an older man. At night we closed off the kitchen with a curtain and my brother Joseph and I shared a bed on the other side. The four girls slept in one bedroom on two small beds and my parents had their own room. When my grandmother - my mother's mother - came to live with us, we built a separate room for her and she had her own kitchen.

In our *shtetl* (village) in Szczekociny, Poland, not too far from Krakow, there were hundreds of families, almost half of them Jewish. But what everyone had in common, Jewish or not, was that they all had only a little money. Compared to most of them, my family was well off. We weren't rich but we never went hungry. Not then, anyway. We did have enough money to pay for two women who worked for us, one to cook and one to clean and care for the kids. All of us went to school until we were thirteen and then we went to work.

Growing up I went to *cheder* (Jewish day school) in the morning. My favorite subjects were math and ancient history. I had many friends and I loved my teachers. Our little school was in the center of town, not far from the main *shul* (synagogue) where I spent the afternoons learning Torah. That was my routine until I turned thirteen and had my bar mitzvah. That was the happiest day of my life. My father Meyer woke me early and we walked to the *shul* together. I don't even remember if it was the spring or fall it was so long ago, but I do remember the colors. The *shul* was filled with men dressed in black capes, their long beards white like the *tallitot* (prayer shawl) draped over their shoulders, while the bright yellow light shone through the windows from outside.

My bar mitzvah was like any usual Saturday morning service with a mix of Hebrew and Yiddish, praying and chanting. When it was my turn to come forward for an *aliyah,* the honor given to recite the blessings before and after the Torah is read, I was nervous. This was a big deal. My father patted my shoulder as I stepped toward the pulpit in my brand new black shoes, and everyone was watching me. Everyone knew my father Meyer. He was an educated man and was the President of Mizrachi, the Zionist organization in our town. He also sang in our *shul* choir. Everyone said he had a voice like a cantor. I had big shoes to fill. When the rabbi nodded to me that I should begin reading, everyone became very quiet.

"Baruch atah Adonai…" The Hebrew I chanted without effort, each word perfect. Halfway through I looked over at my father sitting in the front row, proud and dignified. I smiled and finished the prayer. When I was done, the rabbi and cantor each shook my hand, and so did a whole line of other men in the congregation as I returned to my seat. Everyone congratulated me. It was the biggest moment in my life. I had become a man.

After the service we all drank vodka in small glasses. It made my eyes water and the men laughed and clapped me on the back. We ate sponge cake and honey cake and herring. Later, a little drunk from the liquor and the food, my father and I walked home. Waiting there for us were my family and other relatives who also lived in Szczekociny. Little children were outside playing and the adults were in the house talking and eating chicken dishes and apple cakes. Everywhere you looked there was laughing and joy and most important, love. No one knew it would be one of the last times we would all ever see each other again. From the fifty people in our house that day, only a handful would be alive ten years later.

The Schwartzbaums were one of the largest families in town. My father was one of five brothers and two sisters and all were married with kids of their own. But one of Meyer's sisters almost didn't get married because there was no more money left for a dowry. When her fiancé refused to marry her without one, my father Meyer, who had inherited his father's home, wanted to give it to his sister to use as a dowry.

"But Meyer, you have four daughters of your own," his wife Rivka, my mother, cautioned him. "What are you doing?"

And Meyer replied, "God helped us before, he will help us again."

A few days following my bar mitzvah, I went to work at the family business. My grandfather Asher, my father's father, had opened Schwartzbaum's Lumber when my father was a boy. The lumberyard bought trees from a mill in Prade, cut up the wood, trimmed it and sold the pieces to carpenters who made furniture, cabinets and shelves. When my father took over he expanded the business by taking over the mill and opening a second lumberyard there too.

The lumberyard in Szczekociny was next to a large lake full of fish. My father and I walked by that lake every morning when we went to work. During those walks my father reminded me often that he wanted me to know every part of the business and that was why he had me do every job. I dragged wood until my back was sore. I swept sawdust until my eyelashes were coated. And I learned to price the wood until my head was a jumble of numbers. When I wasn't working I was studying my father at work: how he inspected trees, how he dealt with customers, how he knew the best ways to cut wood so very little was wasted. I also went with him to the bank, listened to what he said and how he spoke when he borrowed money to buy the wood. He was a well-respected man. He was honest and worked hard and I saw that everyone who worked for him loved him. I felt proud to work by his side, especially when he would rest his large, hard workingman's hand on my shoulder and introduce me as his son. We worked day and night together and I learned everything there was to learn about the lumber business.

My older brother Joseph had been the first to work there, but after a few days he said he wasn't interested. Joseph was a scholar and wanted to be a writer, and was the only one of us kids to wear glasses and had his nose always in a book. Our father Meyer understood this and encouraged Joseph to study, and didn't push him to work in the business. Even though he could have used Joseph's help, Meyer would never force anyone to do something he didn't want to do. That was just how kindhearted and wise my father was.

I, on the other hand, loved working with my father. We would leave early in the morning when the sky was still dark and the air cool, and I tried to keep up with his long steps on the short walk to work. It was the same path my father had walked with his father and the same one I thought I would one day walk along with my own son when Schwartzbaum's Lumber was passed down to me.

Since we were a family-owned business, my mother helped with the books. I remember my parents sitting at the old wooden kitchen table under a little light on the other side of the curtain late into the night, papers spread out over the table. There they would try to figure out how much wood they needed to buy, how many people they needed to hire, how much money was coming in, how much was going out, and whether they needed to borrow from the bank. It was always a gamble, but my parents were good business people and always came out ahead.

Meanwhile, my two older sisters, Cesia and Rachel, and my two younger sisters, twins Lola and Cenia, were all seamstresses. They sewed all our clothes and there were always piles of fabric on the chairs, tables and beds. I often went to sleep lying on top of cut up pieces of shirts and pants with pins still sticking in them. And since Joseph refused to have anything to do with their sewing, I was their only model. At night, when I would come home tired and sore from a long day at work, they would come at me with colored swatches and pin them to my chest and back. I was often stuck by their pins and pretended to be annoyed, but I loved every minute. My family was all I knew of the world and being around them was all I ever wanted. I was especially close with my mother Rivka who had developed an overactive thyroid, which made her sick a lot. I was always scared of losing her. On Friday evenings when my father went to the *shul* and my brother and sisters went out to visit with other kids, I stayed inside with my mother. I was worried she might choke on something since we could not turn on the lights on *Shabbat*. Even when she insisted I go out, I refused and stayed by her side. As much as I loved to visit and play with other kids, I loved her more. I got that from my father.

But as smart a merchant and as honest a man as my father was, he did have one fault. Like I said, he had a heart of gold. This came to light when his brother Mendel came sniffing around for a job. Mendel, who had a wife and six children, was always trying to get work but was never able to stick to any job for very long, constantly needing more money to support his family, forever changing to a "better" job, but he never stayed long enough to become successful at the work.

Avram, the oldest of my father's brothers who owned his own lumberyard that sold pre-cut wood, heard of Mendel's dilemma and came over to our house one night.

"Meyer," Avram warned, "don't let Mendel into your business. I did and he cleaned me out financially."

"How can I not help him?" Meyer said to Avram, who had two girls and a son my age. "He's my brother."

So, not only did my father give his younger brother Mendel a job, he made him a partner in the business. Mendel's job was to oversee the lumberyard in Prade. At the lumberyard there was a house on the premises and Mendel and his family moved in there. Sure enough, less than a year after Mendel came into the business, money began disappearing from Schwartzbaum's Lumber.

My parents could not figure out how the money was being lost, and could only think of Uncle Avram's warning. They would stay up very late, night after night, sitting at the kitchen table, adding and re-adding long lines of numbers, and shaking their heads. I had recently turned fifteen and was working at the lumberyard in Szczekociny, and when the money problems came up, my father asked me to move into the house at the lumberyard in Prade and work there. My new responsibility was to watch Uncle Mendel. When he took a step, I took a step. After a short time I finally saw how he was actually stealing money and I immediately went to my father with my report.

In the kitchen that evening, I told him the details of what I found. My father stared at his hands for a while, silent, and shook his head, whether in disbelief or in sadness I couldn't tell. My mother reached across the table and covered his hands with her own, but hers were so small it was like putting a towel over an elephant. After I said "Good night" to them and closed the curtain, they continued to sit for a long time.

The next day my father confronted Mendel. "Where's the money?" was all he said to him.

"What money? I have no money," Mendel replied, and then told my father to go jump in a lake.

"After all I've done for you?" my father replied. It was then my father finally realized what kind of person his brother really was. Left with no other choice, my father demanded that Uncle Mendel go with him to the Rabbi. At that time people went to a rabbi instead of to court. But Mendel refused to go because he knew he was guilty.

Soon after that my father fell into a depression. His business was his life and it was dying in front of him. He had no security to give the banks, and with no bank money to buy trees, he had nothing to sell. He felt he was a failure and watching him made me feel completely helpless. Then I had an idea, which made sense to my fifteen-year-old mind. The insurance company could pay for all the stolen wood that Mendel had taken. After all, we suffered from the crime of Mendel's theft, and wasn't that what insurance was for?

On a hot summer night when Mendel and his wife were out

of town, I played cards with the night watchman, a Pole named Yanich, who also lived at the house at the mill in Prade with his wife and three kids. I brought Yanich a full bottle of whiskey, which I took from my father's pantry, and Yanich was only too happy to drink the entire bottle. When Yanich finally passed out, I went to the back of the house where I had hidden a bag of coal, which I had collected all week from the bakers in town, then took it and went into the lumberyard. It was a little after midnight and the moon was bright. Along the edge of the lumberyard's main building were the stacks of wood for sale. The stacks usually reached to the top of the warehouse, but now on account of Mendel's many thefts, there was only a small fraction of the inventory. I reached into the bag for the pieces of coal and spread them around the wood. I thought the extra coal would make it look like more wood had burned than what was really there. Next I poured gasoline around the coals and lit a match. The wood was dry and it made a fire much faster than I expected and everything burned quickly. I watched for a minute as the fire grew and then ran back to the house where Yanich was still passed out. By the time I had taken a shower and gotten into bed, what was left of Schwartzbaum's Lumber was up in smoke.

The fire department came quickly. One fireman came into the house and woke me up, along with Mendel's children and Yanich and his family, and told us to get out. We all stood outside watching the fire. It wasn't until the morning that we could see the total destruction. Whatever remaining pieces of wood we had had left to sell were now ash, but the main building itself, though scorched, was still standing.

The firemen went over to Szczekociny to tell my father, but he was out of town collecting money from customers. When he returned later that day the firemen told him what happened. My father may have been upset before but now he was broken, his years of hard work lay in ashes under his feet. And worse, the insurance company suspected him of setting the fire, even with his good alibi, and said it would be a while before he could collect any money. I began to feel very worried about my theory of insurance. How could I have figured so wrong? The news that they suspected him almost killed my father. He was such a straight guy that just being accused crushed him.

Losing heart, my father liquidated what was left of Schwartzbaum's Lumber. All the while, I was afraid to say anything.

Meanwhile, my mother Rivka was still earning money running her own home supply business she had inherited from her father. As a girl, Rivka grew up comfortably in Szczekociny. Her family had two maids, one for cooking and one to watch the children. When she was thirteen, she stopped going to school and went to work helping her father with his deliveries. She enjoyed that much more. Together they delivered kitchen supplies like washing powder, linen, soap, and towels to four wealthy landowners and their families who lived in castles on separate estates. These people were Polish politicians and local royalty who had their own cooks, gardeners, house cleaners and even their own school. Each estate had a few hundred people who worked there, tending to the acres of farmland or helping run the household. This was just the way it had been for more than a hundred years.

Sometimes when the landowner customers went hunting, they would skin the carcasses and sell the skins to Rivka's father, who in turn sold them to someone else for a profit. When Rivka's father died, she took over his business. Whatever her wealthy customers needed, she learned how to provide it. She had a good head for business, and she learned to expect in advance what her customers would want.

When Rivka was eighteen she fell in love with my father Meyer Schwartzbaum. The two were both hard workers. When my brother and sisters and I were little we used to help my mother with her work. Sometimes she would buy newspapers and books by the pound from the estates. After Joseph picked out the books he wanted to read, the kids would separate the rest into two piles. Some items were still worth money. Those that had value, my mother sold to stores. The rest, the newspapers and magazines, were sold by the pound to grocery stores. It was like recycling. My mother made steady money by doing this.

But it turns out my mother had been putting all her profits into Schwartzbaum's Lumber, so now, with little or no income from the lumberyard, and her savings also gone, and no insurance money paid, all of us were forced to get other jobs. It was 1936 and I still never told anyone that I had set the fire.

Three of my sisters, Rachel, Cesia and Lola, got embroidery work in Bedzin, a town not too far away. They lived together in a tiny apartment above an embroidery shop. Two of my sisters sewed by hand, and one used a machine. They spent their days making Polish flags with stars and stripes and one large eagle, the national bird, in the center. They couldn't send money home because it took ten weeks to make just one flag and they were paid only when the flag was finished and the money they made was just enough to live on.

The year before, Joseph had moved to Bedzin and lived with cousins so he could be closer to the Yeshiva where he studied accounting and where he worked as a bookkeeper for a bicycle manufacturing company. When Joseph read in the newspaper that a lumberyard was looking to hire someone, he told me to apply. The job was in Ustron, a country community three hours away from Szczekociny that was a vacation spot for tourists. Even though I had never been that far away from home, I went to Ustron. My family depended on it. The job paid 40 *zloty* (about eight dollars) a month plus my room and food. This was a lot then. I lived in a one-room apartment in the center of town. The room had a little light and only a little hot water. It was a beautiful town but I never saw it. I worked every day from morning until evening.

The owner was a German Jew named Freud who owned three other lumberyards in the area, all of which he started from the ground up. While I had learned a lot from my father, I learned even more from Freud. He too bought trees and cut them down, selling the leftover pieces to coal miners, so nothing was wasted. His businesses did very well and soon so did I.

Freud had a son Jack in his early twenties and we became good friends. Jack used to take me with him to nightclubs at wealthy vacation spas in the town where women in their thirties and forties who were married to older men, were eager to meet younger men like me. I was seventeen and to my surprise, a stud.

Freud's wife took me under her wing and treated me like a son. She cooked for me and washed my clothes. It made being away from home a little easier, but not much.

After four months, Freud was so satisfied with my work he put me in charge of one of his lumberyards and doubled my salary. I also received tips. After paying my rent, I now had plenty of money left over which I sent to my parents. I was the only child who made enough to send home. But even though I was busy working and making good money, I was still homesick. When my time finally came for a vacation, I raced home.

I walked into my parent's house on a Friday night and no sooner did I step through the door, I looked at the scene and began to cry. My mother was sitting there in the kitchen, with no electric light on, just two small candles burning on the table, and she was staring into the dark. She looked like she was in a trance. When she first saw me she thought I was a ghost. I asked where my father was and she said without expression, at the *shul*. It was Shabbat after all. I looked around and where there was usually *challah* (bread) left over from dinner, the counter was completely bare. I opened the refrigerator and saw a few onions and potatoes.

When my father came home he explained that they were still waiting for the insurance money, which was being held up because the insurance company was suing him. They still suspected my father of arson. No one ever suspected me. I had such grief over this, but I could say nothing. My "vacation" was very painful.

I went back to Ustron, to my life alone, determined to work even harder to collect more tips so I could send more money home. I worked like a dog and slept only a little. Months later my brother Joseph showed up with good news. Exactly one year after the fire, the insurance money finally came. It was approximately 25,000 *zloty* (about $9,000). My parents and grandmother decided to leave Szczekociny and move to Bedzin. They found a large five-room apartment and all the kids moved back in together. It was a luxury. Everyone was making money, and for the first time in her life, my mother was able to stop working.

My father joined me at Freud's and worked as a salesman, taking orders from coal miners. He worked on commissions, and with his experience and skills as a salesman, quickly became successful. He began buying merchandise on his own from other lumberyards and had it shipped on trains directly to the carpenters. My sisters continued to work as embroiderers, making flags. One flag my sister Rachel made by hand turned out so perfect she sold it for 1500 *zloty* (about $400.) She was a talented artist.

Finally, after a full year, everything seemed to be coming back to normal. Not only were we better off than we had been before, we were together as a family again and the old Schwartzbaum lumber fire and my huge mistake were finally behind us.

Papa: *One time this prisoner got sick. He had diarrhea and couldn't hold on. They took him out from where he worked on the highways, gave him a good meal, and then injected him with poison and he died instantly. Then we had to bury him.*

Felice: *If the Germans were going to kill him, why did they bother giving him a good meal first?*

Papa: *So he should be happy before he dies.*

Felice: *Really?*

Papa: *I like to think that.*

2

The Beginning of the End

I remember that first night, Kristallnacht they call it, because of all the broken glass on the streets of our town. In one day, the Germans destroyed many Jewish businesses and burned down every shul. No one could believe it. We were in shock. I kept hoping I would wake up from a nightmare. It was a wake-up that many decided to ignore, thinking it couldn't get worse. But my brother Joseph knew better. He paid someone to smuggle him to the border and he made it safely to Russia. He had begged me to go with him, but I stayed with my family. If we knew even a part of what was coming, we all would have gone with Joseph to Russia.

By September 1939 when the Nazis invaded Poland, we

realized it was too late to escape. We sent my grandmother to live with my mother's sister Sarah, and she died soon after. Many old people died quickly as if they knew what was coming, as if they knew they'd be the first killed. Our family did not want to be separated again, so my father decided it was time for all of us to leave Bedzin. My parents, four sisters and I all went back to Szczekociny. We did not think Hitler's army would come so fast, but we were wrong.

As we headed to Szczekociny on foot, we saw Jewish spies coming from that direction. They told us that German soldiers disguised in Polish uniforms speaking perfect Polish, had floated down from the sky in parachutes. When they landed, all hell broke loose. Right away they rounded up as many Jews as they could and marched them to the town of Slavkov nearby. They lined them up on the shore of the Warta River, shot each one, and then dumped their bodies into the water. The river soon became known as "The Bloody River."

The spies said we should turn around and go back. My mother and father had wanted to continue to Szczekociny to be with the rest of our family, but we became afraid, so we went back to Bedzin. It was evening when we returned home. We hoped we would be safe but the Germans had already begun taking over. We were terrified to leave our house again.

Weeks went by and we lived like prisoners in our own home, allowed out only to work. The Jews were made to clean the streets. Then Germans, dressed in uniforms with red swastikas on their arms, posted flyers around our town on all the storefront windows and houses ordering the Jews now to wear yellow armbands. We had to buy them ourselves and wear them whenever we went outside. If we didn't - as some in the beginning did not do - the Germans shot them on the spot, no questions asked. Jews were also given a curfew. We were not allowed to leave our homes after five in the evening. Life was changing so fast it was like a dream. A bad dream.

During the day green military jeeps drove through the streets kicking up dust, with microphones attached to their roofs that were all the time shouting propaganda, announcing things like "All Jews look alike. Not like human beings, but like crazy people!" Or "Jews look like cartoon characters." Soon after, cartoons appeared in the newspaper making fun of how we looked. Groups of SS officers were often seen pinning religious Jewish men to the ground and cutting off their long beards, a very sacred part of our Judaism, as it is the Torah's commandment for them not to shave. The men screamed as if their long beards had nerve endings and they could feel each hair being cut. Polish friends I knew for years suddenly hated me. If you met a thousand Poles you'd be lucky to find one good one.

Meanwhile, we heard from Joseph through letters he sent. He had settled into the town of Rostov and got a job as a journalist for the Russian newspaper *Pravda*, the leading newspaper of the Communist Party. Along with the letters he also sent sugar, tea and coffee. But soon his packages came without letters. Strange, we thought, until one day two SS officers appeared at our door demanding my father tell them who was sending packages from Russia and what other secrets he knew. My father was afraid if he said it was his son they would track Joseph down and kill him, so

Meyer didn't answer and they began to beat him. My father begged the SS officers to let him go but they only answered with more beating. Finally my father admitted where the packages came from. Even after his confession they beat him again and left him bleeding and moaning on the ground.

The Germans had taken over the post offices and were opening our packages. At first they let us keep the tea, coffee and sugar, but after the SS officers' visit, those too, were confiscated. No one heard from Joseph ever again.

By November, two months after the war began, the Germans gave orders that all Jewish men between the ages of sixteen and thirty were to report to the center of town. From there they were sent to labor camps where they were forced to build roads. Most every family had been split up and I did not want to go.

We lived on the fifth floor of an apartment building, so when the order to assemble came, I climbed up to the roof and slid down the chimney to hide. The chimneys were a lot wider back then. I would have been safe, but a neighbor, a Jewish policeman named Blum, ratted me out to the Germans.

"The Schwartzbaums have a son who must be hiding," Blum told the German police who were going from home to home.

Then two SS officers barged into our apartment looking for me but could not find me. I heard all this from my hiding spot in the chimney and smiled to myself thinking I'd outsmarted them. But when I heard them threatening to take my mother instead, I came down right away and reported myself to the German authorities.

They sent me to Sosnowitz, twenty minutes away, along with hundreds of other prisoners, mostly Jews. In Sosnowitz we were put into straight even rows, identified, logged in like the lumber I used to sell, divided up and sent off in trucks to various labor camps.

I was sent to Gogolin labor camp. On arrival they gave all of us black uniforms with white armbands that had yellow Jewish stars on the sleeves. There we built entire highways by hand. I was still young and healthy and worked hard. If you worked hard they did not kill you. If you worked hard, you lived. If you could not work, the Germans beat you and if you were lucky, you died right away. I was at Gogolin a year and a half. It was 1941. I was nineteen. I never saw my parents again.

But by a miracle, I did hear from them. My mother was somehow able to send letters and packages to me in the Gogolin camp. I learned that she, my father, and sisters Cesia, Cenia, and Rachel were still living together in the Bedzin ghetto. My sister Lola was sent to the Greenberg camp. Along with the letters, my mother put in any food she could. That food was a godsend. Food was a treasure; even old potatoes or a hard crust of bread gave me energy. Given that I was a hard worker, one of the German commanders in secret gave me extra food and soup, because my hard work made him look good. Since I was eating enough I continued working hard. That, for the time being, kept me safe.

One day while working on the highways, an older Jewish prisoner near me got sick. He had diarrhea. When two SS officers dragged him away from where he was working, you could see the stains on his pants. We all watched but kept working, knowing if we stopped, even for a second to scratch an itch, we'd get a beating. From the corner of my eye I looked in amazement as the

SS officers brought him back to the campsite, sat him down on a bench and served him a good meal. What did this act of kindness mean? Was the war almost over? A wave of happiness, an emotion I hadn't felt in months, swelled up inside me. But it didn't last. After the prisoner finished eating, one of the SS officers injected him with a long needle. Immediately the prisoner slumped over and died. Then the SS officers called for me and another prisoner to come over.

"Bury him," they told us. We lifted the man's limp body off the ground. I held him under the shoulders and the other held his feet as we walked towards the large hole behind the tents where other dead bodies were beginning to pile up. When I looked down, the dead man's eyes stared up at me as if asking, "Why?"

For almost a year the Germans needed men to work on the Russian railroads, which they captured after Leningrad. The railroads needed to be widened so German trains could run on them and – though we didn't know it at the time – also carry us to our own deaths.

Each labor camp was required to send one hundred men to help with the railroads. They wanted only the strongest to be inspected for strength. Many of us were sent off to the Maslovitz transfer camp, a few hundred miles away. Based on that inspection, we were either shipped off to work on the railroads or killed. Since I was still in good shape I was sent to the Ostenzantz labor camp where I worked on the railroads for six months and never once took off my shoes. It was winter in Russia, which meant the temperature usually stayed around zero, day and night. We slept in tents, many dying of frostbite while they worked or even while they slept. More than once I woke up with a corpse lying next to me. Sometimes I was jealous.

At the railroads, the commanders who watched over us were called foremen. The foremen wore yellow uniforms like the men who worked for the Labor department. One in particular, General Ott, who was in charge of the construction of all transportation, told my group there was a treaty between the labor camps and the construction sites that all prisoners must be returned "dead or alive." Knowing they didn't care if we lived or died really frightened me. It was then I knew things could only get worse, but still I was determined to survive. I was young and believed I had a long life ahead, one with a wife and children. This was my dream every day.

After I was there six months, General Ott was killed. He had been good to us but after he died our luck changed. General Spare, a tough commander from the Barbyr concentration camp who came with a reputation for killing many Jews, replaced him. He sent us all back on trains to the Maslovitz transfer camp as promised - dead or alive.

The Maslovitz transfer camp was a disaster. The prisoners were full of lice because we had not washed for several months. Our clothing was taken away, in some cases peeled off our skin, and tossed into heaping fire pits. We were then herded naked, like cattle, into large empty concrete washrooms. Many showerheads were spread around the walls. There was a lot of confusion as prisoners screamed, cried or prayed, afraid we might be in the gas chambers we'd heard rumors about. Then, standing like matchsticks inside a box, we heard a loud gurgling sound.

Was that gas making its way through the pipes? I shivered even though my body was already numb from the cold. There was a long silence. And then... Water. It was ice cold, but we cheered as we bathed. Pieces of soap were passed around and for one moment, one tiny moment, it was a celebration and we laughed. After that shower, most of us still had lice so we were immediately put back in. Even after three cleanings we still had lice, so then they turned on the hot water. Despite the harsh washings, everyone was still itching. The showers were not for our comfort, but to keep us healthy a little longer so we could work for them a little longer.

Not long after our arrival, as a result of the lice, typhus broke out and many died with their eyes open, their last words often being, "Give me a piece of bread and let me die in peace."

We continued to work on the highways for a few more months and when the lice epidemic was finally over, everyone was sent to other camps and Maslovitz was quarantined. Somehow I came out alive from there. I was lucky. It was 1942. I was twenty-one years old.

Papa: *One time two prisoners tried to escape from the Deerfoot labor camp.*

Felice: *Deer foot?*

Papa: *No, Deerfoot. D. I. R. E. N. F. O. T. Anyway, some prisoners from Treblinka showed up and said we should run away because the Germans are going to destroy us and nobody's going to live and we should make eh, what's that word?*

Felice: *A tunnel?*

Papa: *No, we should make, eh, ah rising.*

Felice: *Uprising?*

Papa: *Yeah, uprising. But we were scared. So the two prisoners escaped alone and were caught and hanged.*

Felice: *Do you have another story like that?*

Papa: *Yeah. I have plenty of stories.*

3

"Muscle" Men

My third labor camp was Direnfurt where we built more highways. I was hand picked by SS Officer Lindner who was known as a Horse Counter. At that time Jews were called horses. Direnfurt was a paradise compared to the other camps. I still had a connection with my family and wrote them letters and by a miracle they were still able to send me packages. But now when my family sent me bread, they hid money and gold inside which I used to trade for food with a German commander. Other prisoners started asking me to trade for them, trusting me to trade with the German. They gave me their treasures – silver and gold fillings which they took out from their own teeth, hidden money, old family heirlooms they managed to smuggle – and I came through for them and took my cut in food. Everybody was getting something they needed, but more importantly, I had found a way to survive.

Because of my age and strength I was soon made a *kapo*, a fellow prisoner put in charge of a group of Jews. If they couldn't work because they were too weak, I was under strict orders to hit them. But I could not pick up my hands to hurt them so instead I did the work for them. If I didn't, they would have been shot. And worse, I would have been shot, too. Building highways, laying tar, spreading sand and picking up rocks was hard work, especially on small rations of food. I was always hungry. Even today I can feel the hunger. Eating doesn't make it go away because it's not in my stomach.

One night, asleep in my barrack on a hard plank of wood with my own blanket and pillow, the nicest sleeping arrangement I had since I left home, two new Jewish prisoners were brought into our barrack. They had escaped from the Treblinka extermination camp not far away and were caught. Immediately we all shouted questions at them, hungry for information about our families. But these two men said they knew nothing about lost siblings or parents, only that what the Germans had in store for us was far worse than we could ever imagine.

"The Germans are going to murder all the Jews, every single last one. No one is going to get out alive. We have seen the beginning of the end," said the two men as though they were in a trance. Their words, much like the look in their eyes – empty, with dark circles much deeper than the ones most of us already had - scared us. "We should make an uprising and try to escape."

We could not believe what they said, that we would all be murdered. We were prisoners of war, not an entire people to be slaughtered like sheep. Plus, we did not want to make trouble.

So the two prisoners decided to escape alone, but were caught and hanged in the center of the labor camp for everyone to see. The Germans gathered us around the two dead bodies and shouted, "This is going to be you if you try to run away!" Those two prisoners, it turns out, had only been partly right when they said, "In Treblinka nobody comes out alive." We soon learned it was not just in Treblinka where Jews met that fate.

A few nights later a loud siren blared through the camp and woke everyone up. Despite the harsh conditions of the barracks, sleep - even in the cold - was the most precious part of the day. It was the only time we could escape from the day's nightmares. As the sirens blasted, SS officers ran through the barrack, banging on bed planks and heads with wooden batons, yelling for us to come outside. Shivering, our teeth chattering, we were rounded up in the dark, the freezing wind howling and biting into our unprotected bodies, and ordered to stand around a jeep.

There was a slight commotion as the circle opened and an SS officer stepped into the middle, dragging a Jewish prisoner behind him by his shirt. I recognized the prisoner as one of the twenty men who worked in my group. Seeing him, I realized I didn't even know his name. His hands were tied behind his back with a rope and blood soaked through his torn clothes, obviously from a recent beating. The SS officer stopped next to the jeep. The prisoner was pushed to his knees, his head bowed, either from shame or pain. The SS officer then raised his arm into the air, holding a small object for all to see.

"This Jew tried to steal a potato from the mouth of a pig!" he shouted. In our camp, set up near the kitchen, were pens filled with pigs, which the SS officers slaughtered for meat for themselves. The pigs were fed - as were the prisoners - potatoes.

The circle of prisoners remained silent. The SS officer then used his knee to force the prisoner's head back, and shoved the frozen potato, hard, into the prisoner's mouth. In the clear cold air we heard the crack of teeth breaking. The prisoner's eyes opened wide from fear or from the shock of just having his teeth knocked out of his head, and then the SS officer pulled out his gun and shot the man two times in the face. The prisoner teetered for a moment before falling over like a sack of potatoes.

But this wasn't over.

The SS officer reached into the jeep and pulled out a chain, which he attached to the rope that was around the prisoner's hands. Then the SS officer drove the jeep around and around inside our circle, dragging the dead and bleeding prisoner, the potato still stuck in his mouth.

"You see!" he yelled, a terrible smile on his face. "A pig is more important than a Jew!"

A few days after the pig incident, a tall, blond Romanian SS officer arrived at our camp.

"You're all going to get killed in a few days!" he shouted at our group while we worked. My fellow prisoners immediately stopped working.

"Why should we work if we're going to get killed?" someone said.

I ran over to the officer and said, "Stop telling them they're going to get killed. Why should they work? You're doing sabotage!"

The Romanian SS, upset that I shouted at him, grabbed me and dragged me over to Linar, the camp commander, and told him what I'd said. Luckily I had a good eye by Linar who said, "I will handle it. I will punish him." Linar then took me into his private quarters. I wasn't sure what was going to happen but I braced myself for a beating, either with a whip or a stick, as I'd seen done to others hundreds of times. Instead, Linar sat me down on a chair.

"I will take care of you," he said. "You are going to stay here and work for me. You will clean my apartment and you won't have to go outside and work, because if you do, he will kill you and I can't do anything to stop him."

I couldn't believe my ears. It was too good to be true. From then on, in the mornings I left the barrack and went to Linar's apartment while other prisoners went to work on the highways. I cleaned his room, his clothes and even the pens for his pigs, which he slaughtered himself for special occasions. At night I would go back to my barrack where I had my own bed. The barrack had three wooden cots bunked one on top of another with mattresses made out of itchy straw that poked into you while you slept. Worse, they were infested with lice and fleas, but to me it was paradise. I was eating enough to gain my strength back. But as I was learning over and over again, everything good eventually comes to an end.

When Linar told me he was being shipped off to the Russian

front a few weeks later, I willed myself not to cry. Linar had been the only person to show me any bit of kindness in years.

After Linar left, I went back to working outside on the highways, but no longer as a *kapo*, because I could not hit my fellow Jews. I started wheeling and dealing again with the German commander, trading money and gold for food. This went on for months. Again, I was surviving.

One day, instead of working on highways, I was assigned to work at a labor camp a mile away. I had no idea that we were converting our labor camp into a concentration camp. At the time we only heard rumors about those places. In some way we were preparing for our own deaths. Once the concentration camp was ready, the Germans liquidated the Direnfurt labor camp and sent us all to the Direnfurt concentration camp. I knew I would not be able to take anything with me so I buried whatever valuables I had that could get me another piece of bread. Three months went by and I told the German commander, who I had traded with, where I had buried my goods back in the labor camp, figuring I would barter my "buried treasure" for extra food. The German commander looked, but wasn't able to find my stash and assumed I was lying. Furious for having spent an hour fruitlessly searching, he reported me to an SS officer.

This SS officer dragged me to the location where I claimed the treasure was and demanded I find the goods. I refused to tell him where it was hidden, knowing once he had his hands on it he would kill me on the spot. The SS officer pulled out his gun and put it between my eyes. He pulled the safety and was about to put a bullet in my head, but for some reason changed his mind and took me back to his office. I was taken into the washroom and given a "lesson," fifty lashes with a leather whip on my back and ass. There was lots of blood. Then he dragged me into the shower and poured ice-cold water over me, which stung badly. He was about to give me another fifty lashes when an officer in the "horse" business walked in, reporting that horses were needed to work at another camp. I was ordered to leave the office and was saved from receiving any more lessons.

I went back into the washroom to fix my face, pinching my cheeks so they should look red and healthy, but my pale skin still looked sickly. I reached behind me and swabbed off some blood from my back and rubbed it on my face like rouge, as I remembered seeing my sisters do. Then I raced outside and got in the line. There was no time to plan revenge or even feel revenge. All my energy was used to do what I had to in order to survive. At that moment, even though the pain from the lashes was terrible, I knew I had to look healthy enough to be picked to work – and live. I was chosen right away.

About two hundred of us were taken to the Fintichien concentration camp. After two weeks I learned I had a relative there, a second uncle. I started to cry from happiness. I couldn't wait to see him. He was the first family I had seen since I was taken from my home, over three years before. But it turned out my uncle had become a *muselman*, the Nazis' term for anyone not fit to work. He had given up on life and didn't care if he died. A few days later he did just that.

Thinking I had used up my last bit of luck, I discovered I had another relative in the camp, a cousin named Weitzenberg who worked in the kitchen. He was the son of one of my mother's sisters. My good fortune, I thought. Weitzenberg told me if I came early in the morning he would give me extra food. I asked him to bring the food to me because it was dangerous to go near the kitchen unless you worked there. SS officers were always on guard for prisoners trying to sneak food and shot anyone on the spot. But Weitzenberg demanded I come to him. As scared as I was, I was also very hungry.

Early the next morning I arrived at the kitchen along with several other prisoners, and no sooner did we reach the door, SS officers appeared out of nowhere and began kicking us with their leather boots and chasing us away, shouting, "There's no more food!"

When SS officers handed out beatings, prisoners let their spirits down. You lost your will to live. You gave up. But me, I struggled to hold on. How much more of the war would there be? I told my cousin I would not come to the kitchen again because the SS officers would be there, and that because of the dangers to go to the kitchen, he should instead bring me some food. He told me if I wanted food, I would have to give him money. Turns out my cousin had been stealing food from the kitchen and selling it to other prisoners. Since I had no money (what I had was lost underground), he refused me, his own family.

At that point I felt myself giving up, feeling I could not go on anymore, almost becoming a *muselman* myself. Of everything I had been through and seen, it was my selfish cousin that upset me the most. If my own family would not help me, then who was for me? Was I still being punished for the lumberyard fire? That's when I volunteered myself at the next selection to go to another camp.

Back in the freezing cold, I stood in line, dressed in my thin pants, shirt and hard wooden shoes, along with dozens of other prisoners, waiting to be chosen, like cattle, based on our appearance.

The thing about choosing to leave is that you never knew if where you would be sent would be better or worse than where you were leaving. I was sent to the Gross-Rosen concentration camp in Rogoźnica, Poland. There I began Hell. There I was really hungry. It was 1943. I was twenty-two years old.

Papa: *In Gross-Rosen I worked near the gas chambers.*

Felice: *Were prisoners forced to walk in themselves?*

Papa: *No. They were already dead. My job was to bring over the bodies. It was awful. You know how when wood burns it remains standing? Well, the bodies, the bones, stood up like that in the ovens.*

Felice: *You saw that?*

Papa: *(nods) People who worked near there never survived, because after awhile the SS officers killed those people, so there should be no witnesses. If somebody knows too much, they kill them. Somehow I didn't get killed.*

Felice: *You were really lucky.*

Papa: *(Nods again) Yes, I was.*

4

Dark Smoke

When I arrived at Gross-Rosen, it didn't take long to realize it was a death camp. If I ever imagined what hell looked like, Gross-Rosen was it. There was simply not enough food to feed the prisoners, and SS officers were constantly beating and killing the prisoners, mainly Jews.

I was there only a few months. A few months too many. My job was to deliver the dead prisoners to the crematoriums. I carted them in wagons and left them just outside the entrance where SS officers brought them inside. Chimneys rose out of the roofs and burned non-stop, the air above always thick with dark, oily smoke, the smell of burning flesh was constant. There is no other smell like it in the world.

Not many of the Jewish prisoners who worked near the crematoriums survived, because every three months the Germans killed them off too, so there should not be any witnesses. If somebody knows too much they kill you. Every day I lived in fear of this, but even more, I was afraid with every body I lifted that I might recognize a sister, a cousin, an aunt. I got sick of seeing people burned. I couldn't take it. Meanwhile, the Germans denied they were burning people in gas chambers. They denied it! Things I saw with my own eyes. I saw the bodies in the oven after the flesh had melted away like candle wax, burning like wood. It was beyond depressing. And the smell. As hungry as I was - and I was always hungry - that stench turned my stomach.

But as much as I hated it and was afraid, I worked constantly. At night when my shift ended, I went to work in the kitchen where I peeled old potatoes until late into the night. I was always tempted to steal them but was afraid the SS officers who stood guard, watching us constantly, would kill me. Food was like gold and I did manage to sneak mouthfuls. I only worked there so I could fill up my stomach. I had found another way to survive.

After almost a full year at Gross-Rosen, the SS needed new shipments of prisoners and I was transported to the Braunschweig Drite concentration camp.

Braunschweig Drite was a heaven compared to Gross-Rosen. I worked at the Hermann Goering factory making grenades. The factory was located underground because the Germans were afraid if it was discovered it would be bombed. Every day we lived in fear of the place being attacked from above. I stood all day on my feet putting ammunition into ovens and could not wait to go to sleep each night. And each night when we returned to our barracks after walking through a dark underground tunnel, we would face more challenges.

Our barrack was one long open room, like a garage, with two rows of bunk beds. There were fifty people in one room, but only enough beds for half of us. We not only had to scramble to find a bed to sleep on, we had to find a blanket as well. And if you were lucky enough to get a blanket, you always had to keep an eye on it, because they were constantly being stolen, even while you were sleeping. And if you went to the bathroom in the middle of the night - which wasn't really a bathroom, but a row of raised cement with spaced holes – and did not take your blanket with you, you would return to find it gone. What was worse, every night you attracted lice from all the different blankets. If somebody stole a blanket from me, I had to steal one from somebody else. I lived like this for half a year.

One day in 1945 word spread that the Americans were coming. The Germans were in a panic. They needed to hide evidence and decided to move all the Jews. About six thousand prisoners were gathered from many camps: Jews, Russians and homosexuals, and forced into wooden train cars, bodies pressed up against bodies, bones sticking into bones. We had no idea where we were going or what was in the future for us. It was March, almost spring. I was 24 years old and had been in continuous forced labor for five years.

During the first three days aboard the train we received no food or water. There was very little light and air, only what seeped through the tiny cracks in the rough wood walls. With no place to go to the bathroom, we went where we were, standing up or sitting down. The smell was horrendous. After three days, the train stopped and we were let off. We rushed to get out, but it was difficult since many had died along the way and blocked the exit. Those still alive were forced to drag out the dead and dump them in a pile. Outside, the sunlight was blinding, but the fresh country air smelled wonderful. We were each handed a piece of stale bread and at the exact moment I brought my slice to my mouth, a fellow prisoner grabbed it out of my hand. Hungry as I was, I had not the strength to run after him.

Then, still bewildered from the brightness of the day and my blinding hunger, there was a piercing alarm. The sound filled my head. As the noise screamed down over us, explosions erupted everywhere. The English were bombing from the sky! They had seen the train and must have assumed it was filled with soldiers. They were destroying the trains, railroads, SS officers and prisoners alike. People scattered in the confusion and some, both officers and prisoners, dropped to the ground dead. It was total chaos. The prisoner who had moments before stolen my piece of bread, now lay dead at my feet, the bread still in his grip. I took the piece of bread back and ran for cover.

Night came and it grew colder. People were still scurrying around. I knew I had to get away from the nightmare so I hid in the woods. I had a sliver of shrapnel in my right shoulder and could not get it out. I found a safe place between some trees and fell asleep. I woke a few hours later and looked at my wound. The blood had congealed becoming one solid piece, like chicken fat when left in the refrigerator. The funny part was, I never felt any pain when I was struck.

In the morning as the sun came up, I snuck back to see what was happening at the bombed-out train site. The Germans had recaptured many of the remaining prisoners and made them continue now by foot. From the original 6,000 only about 800 survived. I like to think many got away, but I don't think that's true. From my hiding place deep in the woods I watched the prisoners in that death march walk in silence, their heads hung low. Had I really escaped? Was I free? No sooner had I pictured that possibility, an SS officer appeared above me, the butt of his gun shoved into my back.

"Walk," he told me. But instead of joining the death march, we headed in the opposite direction, going deeper into the woods. We came upon a group of about eighty prisoners lined up in rows standing before a large hole in the ground. A few SS officers were accusing us of looting from the nearby homes. I stood in the back row and watched in horror as the entire first row was shot execution-style. Sticks of men dropped into the pit, their bones collapsing like toothpicks, one on top of the other. They were dead before their bodies even hit the ground.

"I'm a Polish doctor!" yelled a prisoner standing next to me. "I did nothing wrong!"

The half a dozen SS officers holding guns just laughed and ignored his cries. The doctor turned to me and the other men in our row as we stepped forward, closer to the pit, and said, "Come, let's run away. If we stay we will die for sure. This way we might have a chance."

So we took off running, our entire row, all at once. Running zigzag through the forest, I slid in and out of trees so as not to get hit in the shower of bullets that followed us. I kicked off my wooden shoes and ran faster, my feet barely touching the ground. I ran over tree stumps and twigs and leaves and rocks, but felt nothing. When I heard the sound of bodies dropping to the ground behind me, I ran faster. Never did I hear screams of pain, only the rustle of leaves in an otherwise silent forest with people dying quietly.

I'm not sure how many of us ran, I never looked back, but just kept running. I don't know where the energy came from. Again, I was lucky.

I reached the edge of the forest and saw the 800 prisoners, the survivors from the train bombing, all marching in silence. I stopped, shielded behind a tree and caught my breath. I was free, but was that safer? If I was caught, they would shoot me for sure. After a brief hesitation, I snuck into the middle of the moving mass. What other choice did I have? I figured this way I might get some food. This way I had a better chance to live.

We walked for an entire day, many dying along the way, falling to the ground from exhaustion or starvation or a beating or a German bullet. When any of those things happened, no one in line said anything, but instead continued on, stepping right over the dead. If you made a sound, the SS officers shot you. If you stopped, they shot you. Somehow my weak legs carried me.

We finally arrived at another concentration camp and stepped through a metal gate under the sign "Bergen Belsen." My heart was in my throat. This was a place where I had heard many Jews were killed. But just when I felt I could not survive another day, I had a sudden jolt of happiness. I recognized a girl from my hometown! Her name was Helen Wilder. I will never forget her name. I went to school with her older brother. With a new sense of strength, I ran over to her. She stared at me, afraid, as if thinking, "Who is this madman screaming at me?" Finally, after a long hard look, her face softened.

"You have two sisters here," Helen said, "Cesia and Lola."

For the first time in years, I managed to smile.

Felice: *Nana's calling us for dinner. You want to do more tomorrow?*

Papa: *What you want to do?*

Felice: *I have more questions, but I can wait until tomorrow.*

Papa: *All right. Tomorrow. We gonna finish tomorrow. Come, let's eat.*

5

Seventy-Eight Pounds

The first few days in Bergen Belsen the skies always seemed to be gray, the light was gloomy and there was always a hurry in the air. SS officers were stricter, meaner, and quicker to kill. All the prisoners – men and women – were skinny and had no hair. In some cases you couldn't tell the difference between a man and a woman.

After a few days, which felt like months, a miracle happened. I found my sister Cesia. No matter how much weight she lost, how much hair was gone, and how much life had flown out of her, I knew who she was the moment I laid eyes on her. I never hugged anyone as warmly as I hugged her. I wrapped my arms around her thin body and felt I was dreaming and was afraid to let her go, afraid she would disappear.

"Moisheleh!" She touched my face with her hand like bones. Hearing her say my name reminded me I was human, a person, a living soul. For years I was nothing more than a "stinky Jew" or a "horse." Right away I asked her about our parents, but Cesia did not answer.

"Are they all right? Are they alive?" I begged her.

She let out a long breath. "They were taken to a Selection at our ghetto and split up. Men one way, women the other." Cesia's eyes were glassy, but no tears. Who had any left? "Mama wanted to give *Tata* (father) something to wear to stay warm and she held out a sweater. He left his line and walked towards her. When he was a step away..." Cesia's voice faded. My stomach tightened. I knew very well what came next. "An SS shot him in the back. He was dead before he fell to the ground at Mama's feet."

My head started to throb. My father, my hero, murdered. I didn't bother wiping my eyes. I rested my hand on her arm. It was finally all too much.

"What about the other girls?" I asked.

"Lola is here," she said. "But I haven't seen her in weeks. She's on the other side of the camp," Cesia paused. "And right after Tata was killed, I was sent to Auschwitz with Mama and Rachel and Cenia."

I stared at Cesia. Such a lot of news so fast. She'd been in Auschwitz? I heard about the medical experiments done there. SS officers who jumped on pregnant stomachs trying to push out babies, or who cut off men's testicles so they shouldn't be men.

From there, they said, no one came out alive. How had she survived?

"It was the worst place in the world," Cesia said, as if reading my mind. "I saw small children taken by the hands and pulled apart like rag dolls and tossed into a burning fire without even a second glance."

I could tell just by looking at Cesia that along with her illness and protruding bones something was already dead inside her. It was in her eyes. What she had witnessed put a mark on her, made her harder, but in some way, also helped her survive. I wondered how I looked to my sister.

"What about Rachel and Cenia and Mama?" I asked and held my breath, afraid of the answer. Cesia stared out across the cold gray air of the camp, like a picture framed with barbed wire. Tears started to fall on her cheeks. I knew by her saying nothing, that they were all dead. I wondered if they were the lucky ones.

"And about Joseph?" I asked her.

"The last news was that he was still living in Russia." At least it wasn't a report about his death. For many years I chose to believe he was still alive though I never saw him again.

At Bergen Belsen Cesia worked in the kitchen and was friendly with the *kapo* in charge and convinced him to let me work there. My new job was to clean around the outside. In the mornings I woke before the sun was up and went to the kitchen. It was a privilege to get some extra food. Of course, the extra food wasn't much, just a piece of old bread or a hard, usually rotten potato.

On that first day, Cesia snuck me a piece of meat. It had been over three years since I had eaten meat and it tasted like magic. When the aroma first hit I felt I was dreaming. But the moment the meat landed inside my stomach it almost killed me. My stomach had not had in it anything but bread and raw potatoes in a long time. Right away I came down with a terrible case of diarrhea and could barely walk. But like I said, I was lucky. I had found my sister.

Then I developed typhus. Cesia insisted I go to the infirmary, but I refused, knowing the Germans would kill me for sure. They were already trying to get rid of as much evidence as they could because word was spreading through the camp that the war would soon be over. I was too sick to listen to rumors and had only enough energy to get through each day.

Cesia said she would take care of me and tied a kerchief on my head to disguise me as a woman (which wasn't too hard because none of the women had hair), and took me into her barrack where I slept on the floor with her and ten other women. She didn't want me out of her sight. I had diarrhea for days. It got so bad I soon lost all control of my bodily functions and sometimes I went right there in the bed. I was too exhausted to be embarrassed.

But soon I found a new way to survive. In the mornings I hobbled to the kitchen and collected my piece of bread and then hid among the growing piles of dead bodies waiting to be burned or buried. Lying there, day after day, covered in flies and maggots, I imagined the lives of these corpses – fathers, mothers, sisters, brothers. Did I once know any of them? Were any from my town? It was my lowest point. I started not to know anymore whether I myself was really dead or alive. Then the real-life nightmares got worse.

Prisoners, desperate and starving, came by and cut out pieces of flesh from the dead bodies. But the corpses, already rotting, were poisoned from sickness and those prisoners who ate the flesh died right away, collapsing in front of my eyes, sometimes on top of me. The dead piled up throughout the day. I fought sleep as I lay there, constantly afraid someone might try to cut out my flesh, whatever there was of it. Each day I remained in that smelly heap until it grew dark, then I crawled out and went back to the kitchen for a second piece of bread before returning to the barrack.

Meanwhile, as prisoners talked more about the war soon ending, the Germans worked us double time. They made the prisoners drag the corpses to very big holes in the ground and bury them, so that when the Americans came they would not see so many dead bodies. The piles around me slowly got smaller, making my hiding place also smaller.

One day, while lying on the ground, my arms and legs mixed up with the dead, a fellow prisoner pulled on my foot.

"Listen, I'm alive!" I yelled, knowing exactly what he wanted. The prisoner didn't even flinch. He simply dropped my foot and picked up someone else's. It was April 14, 1945. I only know this date because the next day English soldiers arrived and liberated our camp.

I remember that day itself only a little bit. I was lying in my usual place with the rotting corpses and suddenly prisoners began running every which way. As I crawled out from the pile back into the daylight, I saw a crowd of prisoners gathered by the open gate, just standing there. I also stood, not moving, my legs too weak to walk over to them. With no Germans to beat me, to curse me, to threaten me with death, I went back to my barrack until Cesia found me.

"It's over, Moisheleh," she said and kissed my cheek. But I knew better. The war may have been over, but I was a long way from freedom. At twenty-four, I was close to death, and would have welcomed it if it meant peace from my memories.

Over the next couple of weeks, life was starting to change again, but this time, for the better. Because my legs were full of water I couldn't walk, so every day Cesia reported the news back to me. The war was really over. The Germans were gone. The Red Cross had arrived. We would be safe.

The Red Cross set up their camp outside the gates because they feared infection from the outbreak of typhus, but that did not stop these angels from taking care of those who survived. As I lay in the barrack day and night, my mind wandered in and out of consciousness. Had the past five years been a dream? A nightmare? Would I wake up and find myself back in my own bed on the other side of the curtain in our warm kitchen in Szczekociny?

After a few days, Cesia and I went to look for Lola. I could barely walk, my legs so filled with fluid that they looked like balloons, but my will pushed me. We searched and searched but could not find her. I wanted to keep looking but Cesia convinced me to go to the hospital the Red Cross had set up. I finally agreed. I was a man inside a boy's body. I weighed seventy-eight pounds.

Nurses and doctors treated us with medicine and food. Lying in a temporary hospital, my section was roped off because we were so contagious. It took four months until I was a human being again.

Once I was well enough, Cesia found me and broke the news. Lola had died of typhus just two days before the camp was liberated. After surviving five years of suffering! I never got a chance to see her. Cesia and I later looked all over the camp among the dead for her body so we could give her a proper Jewish burial, but we never found her. Even so, I said the *Mourners' Kaddish*, the prayer for the dead.

When I finally got out of the hospital, there was still plenty of recuperating ahead. Even though I received help with my diet, I could not shake the diarrhea for months after.

Aside from the Red Cross, there was a Jewish organization in the United States that supplied food to Survivors, which was what they called us, and told us we would receive money and food coupons from the German government. But during those first months, food and money weren't the first things on my mind.

During all of those terrible years working in the camps and being beaten, I always prayed I would not only survive, but that one day I would be healthy enough to take revenge. Prisoners often spoke about what we would do to the Germans.

One day some Germans came into the hospital. Recognizing the faces of those who, only months before held our lives by the tiniest thread, frightened us, but we were quickly assured the

Germans were now the prisoners assigned to clean the hospital. We were safe, they said, but it turns out the Germans were not.

Every so often, some of the German prisoners went missing. They were beaten and suffocated by the Survivors, their bodies dumped into the piles of rotting corpses behind the hospital. After awhile the German prisoners stopped coming. Even though I had been too weak to do it myself, I had my revenge.

Schwartzbaum Family (left to right): Cenia (note: she is
wearing a "Jude" patch on her dress), Rivka (née
Rappoport), Schlamek Nachemia (Rachel's husband),
Rachel, Cesia and Meyer

Joseph Schwartzbaum

Lola Schwartzbaum

Papa Murray (left) after the war,
with two cousins from Szczekociny

Papa Murray (left) and
Fela (née Gurke)
Schwartzbaum

Papa Murray, Fela
and Rochelle in
Germany

Cesia and Louis
Sillman

Papa Murray and Tosia
(née Jakubs)

Papa Murray in
front of his
clothing store in
Germany

Papa Murray's children, grandchildren and great-grandchildren

Papa: *One time your grandmother got kicked by Mengele.*

Felice: *Joseph Mengele? The Angel of Death?*

Papa: *Yes, she got kicked by him and developed a cyst on the ovaries. After she got pregnant the cyst grew and we thought the baby was going to be defective. Your mother was in the fifth month.*

Felice: *You mean my grandmother Fela was in the fifth month of her pregnancy?*

Papa: *Yeah, Fela was pregnant with your mother. We prayed the baby shouldn't be affected. In the fifth month she had to be operated. We were afraid she was going to lose the baby, but everything came out perfect. They took out one ovary. A woman has two ovaries. They took out one.*

6

Enough is Enough

It was June 1945. Summer. As the color went back into the world, it also came back to our cheeks. We were still living and recuperating in Bergen Belsen. While many had died, there were also survivors. Lots of us. Together we tried to help each other get better from the physical part of what we had just gone through, but no one talked about it; we didn't want to describe ourselves or the animals we had become only just a short time ago. We felt like we were all alive and that's all that mattered. We had lived through the same experience and we also thought that no one would believe how cruel one person could be to another, and we decided it was time to get on with our lives. But before we did there was one thing Cesia wanted to do.

She refused to let the Germans take any more from her than they already had, so she changed her age back five years to how old she was at the start of the war. She said I should do the same, but I didn't. So just like that, Cesia went from being my oldest sister to my youngest.

One day, while still living in the camp, a friend asked me, "Want to meet a nice girl?"

The woman's name was Fela Gurke. To say she was beautiful would be not enough to describe her. She had hazel eyes that looked straight into your heart. Her own heart was unafraid, and honest, without shame or apology. Her deep brown hair was just starting to grow back and her body was quickly regaining its shape. I liked her right away, but since I was dating another woman, she wanted nothing to do with me.

So I broke up with the other woman, but still, Fela refused to date me. But I was persistent and also in love, and little by little Fela got used to me. And in July, when I told her that my sister Cesia and I were going to Nuremberg, I asked Fela to come with us. With both of her parents dead and eight of her ten older siblings also confirmed dead, Fela said she had no reason to stay and agreed to come with me and Cesia. It was, in our own way, an agreement to be engaged; two people who each had almost no one else.

It took three days and three nights aboard a cattle car filled with merchandise to get to Nuremberg. Even though we were safe inside that train car I could still remember my last train ride and every so often I had to stand at the door because I felt like I was suffocating.

After a few months in Nuremberg, Fela and I decided to move together to Regensburg where we heard there were more jobs. Cesia decided to stay because she met a man, Louis Sillman, another survivor who had been hiding in Berlin during the war, and he became her fiancé. Saying goodbye to Cesia was not easy, but I knew it would not be forever.

By the end of the summer, Fela and I were settled in Regensburg in a one-room apartment with separate beds. We told the landlord, a very religious German woman, that we were siblings so she would let us live there together. I was working in a fabric store and made only a little money, but I was also bartering cigarettes on the black market and saved every penny. When I finally had enough money we decided to get married. I bought eggs and butter from a farm for Fela to make cakes and we hired a tailor to make a dress for Fela out of a blanket.

A few days before the wedding, there was a knock on our door. It was my cousin Weitzenberg, the one who had denied me food in the Fintichien concentration camp. It turns out he lived across the street. He was very friendly as though the past had never happened. As much as I swore him dead to me after he refused me food, I had my father's good heart and let him in. I should have known better. The next day he snuck into our apartment and stole our eggs. Needless to say, he wasn't invited to the wedding.

On December 24, 1945, Fela and I were married by a rabbi. The only family members in attendance were my sister Cesia and her husband Louis. It was the first time I had been so filled with happiness since before the war. We were happy to be alive and to have each other. It was just the two of us, alone together.

After the wedding I went into the textile business with another Jewish survivor named Gutteman. The German government had given us coupons to buy a certain amount of material each month at a discount because they wanted to give us the chance to start our new life. We rented a small studio in town and bought and sold bolts of fabric for women's dresses. When the business started to make a good living Fela and I decided it was time to make up for our past losses.

In 1947 our first child, Rochelle, named after Fela's mother Rachel, was born. But Rochelle almost didn't make it. When Fela was five months pregnant the doctor said she might lose the baby because of an unexplained ovarian cyst. But Fela knew exactly where the cyst had come from.

In Auschwitz, Fela had been in charge of a group of female prisoners. One day while working in the hot sun, an elderly woman dropped to the ground. By instinct, Fela bent down to help the woman to her feet, knowing that anyone who stopped working would be killed. As Fela tried lifting the woman, a tall shadow fell over them. The shadow belonged to Joseph Mengele, also known as the Angel of Death. He pushed Fela out of the way, took out his pistol and shot the old woman in the head. Fela screamed as the woman's blood splattered her own face and clothes. Mengele then kicked Fela in the stomach so hard that his heavy boots left bruises. It was that kick, she was sure, that had caused the cyst.

Months after Rochelle was born, I came home one day for lunch to our ground floor apartment. While the three of us sat in our tiny kitchen, Rochelle laughing in her highchair, her chubby cheeks covered in food, a rock broke through the window, landing just inches from the highchair. Shards of glass scattered everywhere.

"Jewish bastards!" someone screamed, followed by the sound of feet running away. It was two years after the war ended. Would another one break out? This was not a new thought. We lived in constant fear of the war happening again and decided right then to leave all the horrors and memories of what we went through and go to America.

The next day we applied for visas. The wait seemed endless. Our sponsor in America was Morris Markusfeld, a distant uncle of Fela's who lived in Brooklyn, New York with his wife Helen, Fela's mother's sister, and their two children. Every few months I sent him money to put into the bank for us, so that when we arrived we would have something to start a new life. Two years later, in 1949 when the visas arrived, we closed up the fabric store, liquidated our belongings, left Germany and never looked back.

Papa:	*Bad things come sometimes at night. You dream, you go crazy, you can't run away. Many times the SS woke us up in the middle of the night and chased us and put lights in our eyes and hit us, you know, with the wire, how do you call it?*
Felice:	*A whip?*
Papa:	*Yes, whips with metal inside. We run always from them.*
Felice:	*They would just wake you up and beat you?*
Papa:	*Yes. These were very cruel SS men. It was the Romanians who were the worst. The Romanian SS had eyes like the devil. They were half-German and half-Romanian. They were monsters.*
Felice:	*And you still dream about this?*
Papa:	*Always.*

7

Fresh Start

We spent ten days on a big ship with about a thousand others. It was a very choppy trip. Many got sick. It wasn't pleasant, but we were all looking to start a new life and we managed to stay healthy. I had no definite plan, no job, just the little bit of money I had been sending. And while we didn't speak a word of English and knew it would be the start of another struggle, at least we would all be together. Plus, we were young and could work.

I'll never forget how I felt when the ship sailed into New York harbor. The Statue of Liberty welcomed us, standing tall like a queen. And the lights from the city's high buildings! It was beautiful. A warm feeling filled my insides. Tears came down my cheeks. I held onto my wife and daughter as tight as I could. We were free people. For the first time in years I felt safe. Stepping off the ship, I kneeled down and kissed the ground.

Waiting for us on the dock was Uncle Morris in a nice suit, his wife next to him, wearing a sharply made dress. They had come to America before the war in 1937 and had two children, a son and a daughter, both much older than Rochelle. Their son was currently away in the army.

We took an underground train to their cramped three-room apartment on St. John's Place in the Crown Heights section of Brooklyn. I had yet to ask for my money figuring it was better to get settled in first.

The neighborhood was marvelous, nothing like we had ever seen before; clean streets, large apartment buildings, several *shuls* and best of all, many other Jews on the street speaking Polish and Yiddish without being secretive. In this free air we felt at home right away. The next morning, I woke to find Morris sitting at the kitchen table. I asked if he would take me to the bank where he had been depositing my money, but Morris just rested his head in his hands. I felt my stomach tighten.

Uncle Morris had not been putting my money in the bank, but hiding it at home. And when his son had last been home on leave, he had taken half of the money and spent it on his girlfriend, a German woman he met while serving in the army who he was planning on marrying.

"A German!" Morris cried. "Can you believe it?" Then he told me he had sat *shiva* for his son, who he said was now dead to him. I was shocked. Not only because of the lost money, but because a family member had turned against us. So, on my second day in America, I set out in search of a job and an apartment.

After two weeks, I found a room for rent in an elderly Jewish woman's apartment on East 7th Street and Avenue C in Brooklyn. We shared the kitchen and had only one room that was big enough for our bed and a tiny one for Rochelle. But it turns out the elderly woman was crazy and one night made me stand in front of the bathroom door and watch in case something happened while she was in the tub. I felt like a slave. We would have left right away, but the old woman's son kept assuring me, saying, "Don't worry, my mother's going to die soon and you'll get the apartment." Apartments were very hard to come by in those days. But after that bathtub incident, I thought I would suffocate first if I stayed any longer, so after only one month, we left.

Luckily I found another apartment. This one was on Bergen Street in Flatbush. A friend of Morris's helped me find it. It cost $45 a month and it was all ours. We had a kitchen, a bedroom and a living room. This was a paradise. But even though we were far from the horrors of the war, the memories still haunted us in our minds. Many nights one or the other of us woke crying from nightmares. You try to knock it out of your head; you think about other things, you tell yourself you no longer have to be afraid, that you are free. But it didn't matter; we were still often prisoners in our own minds.

I got a job working in a sheet metal factory on Houston Street in Manhattan and made 65 cents an hour. The work was very hard and the conditions were terrible. One day Fela came by to see me and became very upset when she saw how hard I was working and sweating and bending the metals. She told my boss she needed to speak to me for a minute, but the boss said I wasn't allowed to take even a five-second break. The next morning Fela wouldn't let me go to work.

"We didn't come to America to kill ourselves," she said. She was a gentle person, but could also be very firm. She was like a real aristocrat, with quiet strength. So I quit and went out looking for another job.

I then learned about a small group of survivors from my hometown of Szczekociny, right there in Brooklyn. It was so wonderful to talk about the good times before the war with people from home. Through them I learned that I had an uncle, Sam Schwartzbaum, who owned a clothing manufacturing factory in Manhattan. Again, I thought, luck was on my side.

I took the subway to his factory in the city and introduced myself. My English had been getting better and I was adjusting well to America. I told Sam he should teach me the business so we could keep it in the family. Sam told me I would first have to take classes and learn how to sew. So I did. For three months I went to night school after working all day. When I went back to Sam, he said he was having trouble with his union and could not hire me. I was in shock, another relative turning his back. I didn't want to see him after that.

With my new skills I landed a job sewing uniforms for American soldiers for 65 cents an hour. After three weeks the company went out of business and I never got paid. Then I got sick.

Suddenly I was losing weight even after eating several sandwiches every day at lunch. Like that I lost twenty pounds. Turns out I had developed an overactive thyroid, just like my mother had.

A doctor named Louie told me the operation would cost $1,500. I told him I had no money, just Blue Cross Blue Shield, but he didn't accept that insurance. I went to another doctor, this one a Jewish American named Teller, who said he would take the insurance and not to worry about the cost, saying he would get a tax write-off.

While I was recuperating in the hospital after Dr. Teller's operation, friends of mine from the Szczekociny Society had asked my Uncle Sam how his nephew was doing. Sam had not known I was in the hospital, so when he learned this, he came to visit. He walked in wearing an expensive suit, handed me an envelope without saying a word, and went outside to smoke a cigarette. Fela was with me and I told her to open the envelope. Inside was a check for $100. We needed the money badly, but I didn't want his charity so I ripped up the check, stuffed it back inside the envelope, and Fela put it back into Sam's coat. A month later I saw Sam at a party.

"Why'd you give me the money back?" he asked.

I looked him in the eye and said, "All I asked you for was a job, never charity."

Weeks after the operation, when I was feeling like myself again, I went back to Dr. Teller to pay him. It would have been all our savings. But Dr. Teller refused to accept it and just patted me on the back and told me he was glad I was all right. A few weeks later Dr. Teller died in a car accident. The man who saved my life had lost his own.

When I was fully recovered I got a new job sewing linings into seams of military uniforms in a large factory on Dekalb Avenue in Brooklyn. I made $2.00 an hour. This was very good money. I got Fela a job there and she worked half days doing finishing work. We were starting to make a living and we sent Rochelle to kindergarten for the whole day for $2.00 a week.

Even though everything was finally going well, my brain was always on high alert. And for good reason. Our boss Joe, a heavy man, was mean. This, along with Fela's sensitivity, was not a good combination. One day Joe started yelling at Fela, ordering her to work faster. He didn't bother any of the other women who were mostly black and Hispanic because they gave him lip right back. But Fela never argued back. From where I was working, under the shine from the fluorescent lights, I could see that Fela was upset. I was afraid it could get out of hand so I rushed over.

"Can't you respect the lady?" I said to Joe. He yelled for me to get back to work. Angered, I grabbed a pair of cutting shears and threw it at him. They landed inches away from him. "The hell with this job!" I shouted and turned to Fela, who looked deeply frightened. "Let's go home. He shouldn't talk to you like that."

On the way home Fela said, "Why'd you do that? We were making a living."

I put my arm around her and said, "I will find something else."

Right away I started looking for a business of my own since we hadn't had any luck working for anyone else. In the newspaper I saw an ad for a grocery store for sale on President Street in Brooklyn. I knew nothing about running a grocery store, but I had learned a lot about running a business from my parents. It was 1951. Fela and I agreed it was time to take a chance.

Papa: *One time in the camps, just before Yom Kippur, we paid an SS officer with money to let us pray to God that day. But after we started praying, a bunch of SS sons of bitches barged in and started shooting at us. We prayed to God and God didn't listen to us.*

Felice: *You still believed in God even after all the killing and suffering?*

Papa: *Eh. (Nods)*

Felice: *Do you still believe in God now?*

Papa: *Listen, you get in trouble, you start believing. What we went through there was plenty miracles that I survived. I weighed seventy-eight pounds, but I survived.*

8

The Past is Still Present

Rosen, the owner of the grocery store located near an orthodox synagogue, said the business took in $600 a week. This was a lot of money. I figured after paying all the expenses, I would take home about $120, enough to save to buy a home. But I was a greenhorn and the man who sold it to me turned out to be a thief.

Rosen taught me everything he said I needed to know; how to work the cash register, how to run the books, and how to slice the deli meat. He introduced me to the vendors who delivered the goods and to the neighborhood locals who shopped there. I learned to inspect produce, deal with suppliers of canned goods and bulkie rolls and toilet paper, and how to price foods to make a profit. After two weeks, I felt ready for business. But after Rosen left (he moved out of state), something wasn't right. The store was not taking in as much money as it had been when Rosen was there. For some reason I was only making $400 a week. A big difference. Every night after working twelve hours at the store, I would come home and sit at the kitchen table and go over the receipts. Many nights Rochelle would sit on my lap while I added numbers over and over. Fela looked at them too, but neither of us could figure it out.

Then one day the bread delivery guy, dropping off his shipment, asked how I was doing. I confided in him that I was having financial problems.

"Rosen was a dishonest guy," he said. "Before he sold you the store, he said to me, 'That Schwartzbaum knows nothing and won't stay in business long.' I don't think Rosen made a profit in years."

It turned out that Rosen had doctored the receipts. There was no use going to the police, Rosen was long gone. I had to come up with a way to make more money, to get the customers into the store. All night I lay awake thinking what my parents would have done. One thing I knew for sure, they would not have given up. And neither would I.

The next morning I got up earlier than my usual five a.m. alarm and took the bus to the store. I went around the neighborhood and introduced myself, bringing milk and saying I would deliver it to their homes in the morning. They were delighted. I figured when they came in to pay for the milk at the end of the week, they would buy other things. Sure enough, I was right. Soon I began taking in even more than $600 each week. I worked from five in the morning until eight at night every day. Life was beginning again.

Fela, when she could, worked in the store with me. It was so nice to be back in a family business. Even Rochelle, when she was only six, would deliver groceries on her way back to school after she came in for lunch.

Soon Fela found herself pregnant with our second child, a son. With the family expanding, we decided to move closer to the store.

In 1953, Sidney, named after Fela's father, was born. What we thought would bring joy, instead brought hardship. Sidney was born very sick. From the start he had a high temperature of 104 degrees, which lasted on and off for six weeks. The doctors said he had meningitis and kept him in the hospital the entire time. Fela went every day and night to see him and read everything she could about the illness so she could understand what the doctors were telling her. Unfortunately her fear of losing Sidney triggered other memories, ones she had tried to forget; those we all tried to forget.

It was good luck that Sidney recovered and everything was back to normal. Business was good, the kids were healthy, and Fela's nightmares had lessened. For the first time in years, smiles actually came easily from her.

When Sidney was six years old, he too made deliveries from the store, and one day he brought groceries to a teacher named Blumfeld. Mrs. Blumfeld lived on the sixth floor of an apartment building and the elevator had been out, so Sidney carried the heavy bags up all six flights. When Mrs. Blumfeld gave Sidney a two-cent tip, he said to her, "I walked up six flights and you only gave me two pennies? You should have at least given me a penny a flight." Then he handed her back the two pennies and said, "Here. I guess you could use the money more than I can."

On his way back, Sidney stopped in the candy shop next to the store. Sidney had been a picky eater and was very skinny and Fela would often treat him to malted shakes. It was there, on a bar stool, sipping his shake, Sidney told the owner, Mr. Silverstein, about his encounter with Mrs. Blumfeld. Later, when Mr. Silverstein told me about the two-cent tip, I knew my son had inherited my father's heart of gold and sense of fairness.

But just as life had begun to settle for us, Fela fell into a deep depression. When we had been living in Regensburg, Fela found out two of her sisters, Franka and Mania, were still alive. Fela had been a Change of Life baby when she was born in 1924. Her mother was almost 50 years old when she gave birth to Fela. Franka, the oldest, who was twenty years older than Fela, had moved to Paris before the war, and survived by hiding in the countryside with her husband, while they hid their two daughters in a Catholic school. And Mania, who Fela had been very close to before the war, had survived Auschwitz and then went to directly to Paris to be with Franka since she thought the rest of her family was dead.

Before Fela, Rochelle and I left Germany for America, Franka and her youngest daughter Bernadette, who was a few years older than Rochelle, came to visit us. We considered moving to Paris, but after that rock-throwing incident, wanted to get as far away from Germany as we could.

Years later, after we were settled in Brooklyn, Franka came to visit us in the middle of the summer during a heat wave. Fela and I had insisted she come to the Catskills with us even though Franka said she wanted to see the sights of New York City. After a day or two in the Catskills, Franka heard that someone was heading back to the city and so she left. After that Fela felt very guilty, feeling she had failed her sister. Her sleep was constantly interrupted with nightmares about her years in the ghettos and camps. Many nights I rocked her like a baby until she fell back asleep. But eventually her dreams crept into her waking life.

At the beginning of the war, Fela, her father, her sister Mania, and Mania's three-year-old identical twin boys had been separated from the rest of the family in the Lodz ghetto. The boys were unusually beautiful and everyone who saw them could not take their eyes off them. Soon after, Mania was taken to Auschwitz and the last thing she said to Fela was, "Take care of my two boys." Fela promised she would.

In the Lodz ghetto they got only very small rations of food. Fela's father, who was a big man, would beg Fela for part of her bread. And though he had lost a lot of weight since the war began, his body still needed more food. Fela often gave him a portion of hers, but never the entire piece, for she needed it too. When her father eventually died of starvation in the ghetto, Fela felt guilty about that, believing that if she had given him more of her bread, he would have lived.

Now Fela was left alone and responsible for Mania's twin boys. Weeks after her father died, two SS officers stormed into

Fela's room and grabbed her two nephews. She screamed and one of the SS officers struck Fela and pushed her down. As she fell, crying, she watched helplessly as the SS officers took away the two frightened boys. She never saw them again. No one ever did. Not a day passed where Fela didn't feel guilty for not saving them.

Fela never saw her sister Mania again. Mania survived but could not face Fela with her silent accusation. Fela felt tremendous guilt for the death of Mania's two sons. It was all these memories from her past that began to invade her present.

With all of this blame within her starting to come out, Fela became a different person. I begged her to see a psychiatrist but she refused. Fela was afraid of doctors.

When Survivors came to New York City they were required to see specific doctors who determined if we were eligible to receive *Wiedergutmachung* (reparations) from the German government. The decisions were based on our health and mental state. I was immediately deemed healthy and therefore did not qualify. Fela, on the other hand, had her decision based on something else.

The first American doctor she went to in Manhattan told her to remove all her clothes, which she did. Then, instead of examining her, he started touching her intimately. At the time there was no such thing as "sexual harassment." Frightened, Fela ran out of the examining room. When Fela told me in the waiting room what happened I bolted into the doctor's office and threatened to kill him. Someone called the police. The police came and were about to arrest me, but the doctor told them to let me go, as he knew he was guilty. Soon after, the doctor 's report called Fela "healthy and mentally stable" even though she clearly was not. Not receiving the pension was the least of our worries. That doctor's behavior not only kept Fela from seeing other doctors, but also triggered more war memories, which she had tried to forget.

For weeks, the children and I watched Fela's behavior and moods grow worse, until finally I convinced her to see a therapist. The first one she went to, a Dr. Perlmutter, lived a few blocks from the store. He suggested having another baby would make her depression go away.

In 1959 Fela gave birth to our third child, Mark, who we named after my father Meyer. When Mark came into the world he brought with him pure happiness that seemed to make Fela's depression melt away. Now busy with the baby, Sidney, and Rochelle, Fela seemed her old self again. But that happiness lasted only four years. After that I started to notice tiny cracks in Fela's moods. Her depression would appear out of nowhere, only this time it was even worse.

Fela agreed to go back to therapy, but it didn't seem to help. One day she became violent. My sister Cesia was over and Fela tried to jump out of a window of our fifth floor apartment. Cesia, who was smaller than Fela, physically tried to restrain her as much as she could, while yelling, "You have a husband who loves you! You have three beautiful children who need their mother! The war is over, you are safe and okay now!"

A neighbor, hearing the screams, called the police. The police came and tied Fela up. Rochelle came home shortly after and saw the sea of police cars and the flashing blue lights and knew something was wrong. In the middle of a crowd of people, Rochelle watched as the police took Fela to King's County Hospital in Brooklyn. She could do nothing.

The next day I went to see Fela at King's County and found her lying on the floor, her cheek against the dirty tile floor. I could have died. Seeing my wife, this beautiful woman who I did not even recognize, was like a knife through my heart. I stormed over to the nurses' station.

"I want her out of here! Take her to Gracie Square!" I demanded. Gracie Square Mental Hospital on East 76th Street in Manhattan catered to the wealthy and was very expensive, but I didn't care.

Midway through Fela's month-long stay, Rochelle took a day off from her classes at Brooklyn College and went into the city to visit her mother. When she arrived at Gracie Square, Rochelle was herded into an airless waiting room and sat with other families waiting to see their loved ones. During those months Rochelle was close to tears all the time. She didn't want her mother to be sick. She didn't want to be there at the hospital. She didn't want to be part of that world. When Rochelle was finally allowed in to see her mother, Fela actually seemed very good. She introduced Rochelle to everyone saying, "This is my beautiful daughter Shelly," the name her high school friends had begun to call her.

During her time at Gracie Square, Fela had been making art and surprised Rochelle with a nature scene she had painted with a cat in the picture. Rochelle had had no idea her mother could even paint.

After two weeks of treatment, which included shock therapy in which they also gave her experimental drugs, Fela came home. She was a new person. She was wonderful, cheerful and most important, healthy. I surprised her with a new bedroom set because I wanted to make her feel good. And she did. That first night home she made salami and eggs, the kids' favorite meal, and she seemed so happy. The kids started to relax and tried to forget their visions of seeing their mother acting terrified and paranoid. Fela now seemed a whole new person. Soon we were a family again.

The first thing Fela wanted to do was have a party to prove to her friends that she was well. We all told her to take it easy and relax, but she was very firm about having that party. She nearly killed herself cooking for the 50 guests, but she wanted to show everyone she was normal. And for the next six months she was.

But after that Fela started slipping back. Any hope I had of the treatments personally wiping away the horrors of the Holocaust was gone. The drugs the doctor had prescribed seemed to make her behavior worse. She had wild hallucinations. She thought that I, the one person in the world who loved her more than anything, was going to hurt her. She stopped trusting our friends and neighbors, and began having stronger flashbacks from the camps. I often wondered how some of us, our friends who had also been in camps, like us, could put aside these memories, and Fela could not.

One beautiful spring day, Fela rushed into the store looking upset. Something was off in her expression; her mouth was tight, her eyes were wide and frightened. She began yelling at me about cheating her, right in front of the customers, and they looked more frightened than Fela did. I was behind the deli counter slicing pastrami, so I stopped, wiped my hands on my apron, and came out from behind. While Fela continued to yell, I smiled at the customers and assured them everything was fine and escorted Fela down an aisle to the back. Standing near a stack of boxes filled with canned goods waiting to be put on shelves, I asked her, my voice as soft as I could make it, like the doctor's instructions, "What's wrong?"

Fela seemed to inflate with each inhale. She shoved my hand from her arm and shouted, "I was on my way to the Laundromat to pick up the clothes when I realized the five dollar bill you gave me this morning was counterfeit. Do you want me to go to prison?"

Tears formed behind my eyes and I wiped them away with the back of my hand. I knew the customers were waiting, but that didn't matter to me. My wife was crumbling in front of me and I had no power to help her. I felt completely helpless, like I did in the camps – my life was not in my control.

I swore to her the money was real, but she was not convinced and ran up the aisle and out of the store. I stood for a moment, unsure what to do. Seeing Fela like that, coming apart, hurt me terribly and the fact I couldn't help her, hurt worse. I returned to the front and took my place behind the deli counter and finished slicing the meat. I don't remember any more of that day at work.

Fela went home to our three-bedroom apartment on Montgomery Street in Crown Heights. There she cleaned the house from top to bottom.

Meanwhile, Mark, a month before his sixth birthday, had gotten off the school bus and not finding his mother waiting, felt that something was wrong. His fear grew as he walked the few blocks home and up the steps to his apartment. He might have been just a little kid, but he was born to a woman not in her right mind, a woman whose mood could change instantly when a bad memory appeared, a woman so depressed that whatever fear she carried inside her, she passed on to her unborn child.

Panicked and crying, Mark pressed on the doorbell until his body began to shake. "My mommy's dead! My mommy's dead!" He shouted that over and over until Rochelle arrived home, about an hour later. She wrapped her arms around her little brother to calm him.

"Everything's okay," she told him.

But everything wasn't okay.

Rochelle and Mark walked into the apartment and together saw their mother, right in front of them, inches away, hanging in the kitchen doorway. They froze for a moment, not believing their eyes. Their mother, the woman with the beautiful singing voice, had hanged herself on Sidney's chin up bar, which he had received as a gift for his twelfth birthday just three days before.

Rochelle screamed. A neighbor ran over and helped take her mother down. Rochelle tried giving her mother mouth-to-mouth resuscitation. And even when the EMT's tried to take her mother's lifeless body away in the ambulance, Rochelle clung to her, not wanting them to take her, knowing when they did that would be the last time she would ever see her mother. Mark, who had witnessed this all, sat whimpering, even as Rochelle held him tight and by instinct, had put her hand over his eyes as he continued to shake.

It had been around two in the afternoon when Fela had come by the store in a rage. At 5:30, when Rochelle called me at work, I knew from her tone that something was wrong.

"Come home quick, Dad," was all she said. But I knew. Usually it took me ten minutes to come home. I was there in two. Fela, my beautiful wife, my life, had killed herself.

Sidney was still at Yeshiva and we asked our dear friend, Roslyn Storch, to pick him up and tell him that Fela was very ill and in the hospital and "may not make it." He had been extremely close with his mother and we were afraid to tell him, thinking it would be better to prepare him rather than shock him with the immediate truth. Sidney went to Roslyn's house and stayed up all night wrapped in a prayer shawl and *tefillin* praying for his mother. Roslyn, who had lost her own mother as a very young child, later told us it broke her heart to watch Sidney pray for a miracle she knew would not happen. The next morning I went to pick Sidney up and take him to the funeral. He knew from my expression what I was going to say before I said it. The kids had been through so much with their mother's illness, they had come to expect tragedy.

So, as Sidney looked at me with his innocent eyes, hoping for good news, I wanted to tell him anything but the truth. Instead I said, "Today we lost a diamond."

Sidney cried for three days. His mother was his world. Not a day went by that Fela wasn't showering him with kisses or pinching his thighs and praising him.

After Fela's death I took on the task of being both a father and mother. I rarely saw the kids during the week because I worked such long hours, but on Sunday nights we always ate dinner together and watched "Bonanza" on TV. "Bonanza" was about a father raising three children on his own, similar to what I was trying to do. Those nights were the only time the kids seemed genuinely happy.

For years, we never told any of our friends or even family how Fela died, but many of them knew, especially the Survivors, who saw in Fela, I think, what could have been their own fate. We told people she had died of a blood clot. And in the time before her death, when she was going in and out of treatment in the hospital, we made up other lies; that she was having her gallbladder removed or a cyst taken out. There was so much shame in mental illness and suicide that we just wanted to cover it up. I didn't realize that for our friends, the lies were okay if it helped.

The years following Fela's death were very hard for the kids, especially because of the secrets they thought they had to carry. Also, losing their mother, they thought they could lose their father, too. I had aged a good ten years in that first year following her death and had lost most of my hair. And what hair I had left turned gray.

One year after Fela's death, almost to the day, Sidney had his bar mitzvah at the Rabbi Frankel Synagogue, the orthodox temple next to the store. I was so proud of him knowing how hard it was, especially so near the anniversary of Fela's death, and I told him, "Your mother's looking down on you." But the one who was actually looking down on him was Rochelle. Women in that synagogue were kept separate and divided from the men in a room above. They had one small window overlooking the sanctuary that had a veil over it, but Rochelle pushed it aside because she wanted to see her brother. She too was very proud of him. Sidney, in his true fashion, had fully memorized his entire Torah portion.

During that time I tried my best, but it was hard to take care of the business and the family. I reapplied for the German pension thinking if I got some extra money, I might be able to cut back and work only twelve hours a day instead of fifteen. I went to an American lady lawyer who gave me the paper work and said I had to go to Israel and reapply in person. So in 1966, after a year of mourning, I took the kids on a trip to Israel with the thought of moving there.

We visited in Tel Aviv with a cousin of mine from Szczekociny. I also saw an old friend from my hometown who was now a widow with two kids. She wanted me to marry her and move to Israel, but I said no. Not only was there the language barrier, but she too suffered from depression and I couldn't go through that again. Right before we returned home, my paper work was accepted and I was cleared to receive a pension, however it was only thirty-five percent of what I was entitled to.

About two years after Fela died, I went on a date after work. I purposely didn't tell the kids, because I knew they still missed their mother very much. Usually I was home at 7:00 each evening, but when I didn't show up, Rochelle and Sidney were beside themselves. Having gone through what they did with their mother, they immediately thought the worst; either I'd been held up and shot at the store or hit by a car and killed riding my bicycle home. At 9:30 they called the police. When they were told there were no reports of any accidents, Sidney rode his bike to the store. When he saw that the gate was locked and everything looked fine, he rode home along a different avenue looking for me.

I finally arrived home at 11:00 and found Rochelle and Sidney sitting by the door looking very pale.

"Why didn't you call? We were sick with worry!" Sidney yelled. He was fourteen, but was acting like the parent. "Why'd you do that to us?"

I just looked at them and shook my head. "I'm sorry," I said. "I met a woman and didn't want to tell you."

"What, better we should think you're dead?" Sidney seemed to have taken Fela's death the hardest. He missed his mom so much and didn't deal with the size of his loss and couldn't cope with the reality that I was seeing another woman. For years he carried a lot of anger inside him.

In March of 1968, Rochelle married Richard Cohen and moved to Massachusetts. One month later, as a surprise to everyone, I married Tosia Jakubs who I had been secretly dating. I had kept it a secret from my kids figuring I would wait until Rochelle had moved out, thinking it would be hard for her, the oldest, to see someone replacing her mother.

Tosia was also a Survivor, as was her first husband, who had recently died from cancer. Her daughter Edith was already married and her son Bert had one more year of high school, so he stayed in Worcester, Massachusetts and lived with a friend when Tosia came to Brooklyn.

It was a big adjustment for all of us. Tosia missed her kids and my sons missed their mother. Mark, now nine, was constantly afraid every time I left the house, worried I wouldn't come home and found comfort in food. And Sidney, once a straight-A Yeshiva student, would disappear for hours. He would often head up to the Bronx to my sister Cesia's apartment where he found comfort with her and her husband Louis and their two sons, Max and Joseph. But one Friday afternoon, just before Shabbat, Tosia called me in a panic.

"Come home right away. Sidney's acting wild!"

By the time I closed up the store and came home, Sidney had run out. I spent hours wandering the streets looking for him and finally found my middle child lying on a park bench. I carried him home and held him as he lay crying. I knew Sidney had never dealt with the guilt he felt over his mother's death, often saying if he had only never asked for that chin up bar for his twelfth birthday his mother would still be alive.

Sidney eventually dealt with his anger and emotional confusion and went back to school and took the entrance exams for three city jobs. He aced every one. Sidney, like me, had found a way to survive.

But none of us could have survived without Tosia. Those early years of our marriage were no picnic for her and that was partly my fault. She didn't know what she was getting into. She always tried her best, but didn't understand the boys' fears. And why would she? It wasn't until a year after we were married that I told her about the suicide. But Tosia didn't know the words "give up." She was strong and determined and that's why I loved her. And even though the environment was difficult for everyone at first, we worked together to become a family. Soon they were no longer "my kids" or "her kids" but *our* kids. We worked together at home and in the store, day after day. Tosia and I, whenever we needed each other, were there. Even now, after forty-two years of marriage, we still take care of each other.

At eighty-six I got cancer in one kidney. When I first heard the word cancer I was very scared. I felt more afraid of the cancer than the Nazis. At least if I worked hard in the camps, I had a chance to survive. But with cancer it's out of your hands. I was told I had to have the kidney removed. Tosia seemed more scared than I. She has been taking care of me all these years and didn't want to lose me.

On the day of my surgery, Rochelle, Sidney and Mark were there for her and me and each other. After the doctor removed my kidney, he wanted me to have chemotherapy, but I refused. I didn't want to live out the rest of my life feeling sick. Sidney suggested I take a special herb that a friend of his researched and took for several years, which cured his cancer. I thought it couldn't hurt and would make me less weak than chemotherapy. I am still taking it and the tumors have shrunk and not spread and I feel terrific. Hitler didn't kill me and I didn't want to let cancer kill me either. I try not to dwell on why I survived and others didn't, but just to continue to be thankful.

I am very close with all our children, grandchildren and great-grandchildren, who I call my "dividends." Each one reminds me of the family I lost and fills me with happiness knowing that because of my survival, I was able to bring more family back into this world. And to that I say, thank you.

Papa: *Is the book almost done sweetheart?*

Felice: *Yes Papa. Soon.*

Papa: *I'm getting older. I want to still be here when the book comes out. I'm eighty-eight. I'm not getting any younger. I want I should have another three years. That's all. Feigela, I love you.*

Felice: *I love you too, Papa.*

Epilogue

I've been listening to Papa tell me his story since I was in college. Never once did I imagine that when he finished telling it to me, it would become my story.

In the beginning, Papa's stories were sporadic. His brain was like a sponge full of memories, and as they poured out, each one triggered more. Dates and details came over time, some of which he knew very well, others were fuzzy. The names of the camps and the names of SS officers he seemed to have tattooed on his brain. Often I would ask him to repeat a story more than once, like the one about the Jewish prisoner who stole the potato from a pig, because I couldn't comprehend that one human being could do that to another. But Papa, his face devoid of emotion or judgment, would just nod his head as more stories rolled off his tongue.

During the many hours we sat talking about his life, whether we were in Boca or Brooklyn, Papa's eyes would glaze over and he would disappear, delving into the past, suffering a second time through horrible memories, for the sole purpose that I should hear and tell his story.

Over the years, whenever we spoke on the phone, he would ask, "How's the book?" For years The Book was something I was doing for Papa, but that changed in 2008 when I went to Poland and visited Auschwitz and Szczekociny, the town where Papa grew up. After that trip I knew that writing The Book wasn't just for Papa's sake, but for mine, for my sisters, my parents, my cousins, my aunts and uncles, nieces and nephews, and for all who need to know.

There are stories in this book my grandfather has never spoken of, ever, even to his own children, afraid of burdening them with the truth. He did not know that by keeping things secret, he was holding onto the pain. Like with my grandmother Fela's suicide. He, my mother, and both uncles had made a silent pact to never discuss it. My mother too, had buried those memories right alongside her mother.

In 1999 I wrote an opinion column about my grandmother's suicide for the *New York Daily News*. And my mom, usually my biggest fan who forwarded copies to all her friends, found herself in a quandary. After my column came out, nationally, she had no choice but to face the truth. So, using my column as the stimulus, she began speaking about it with her friends, friends she'd known for decades. Shortly afterwards she thanked me for helping her rid herself of the shame she'd been carrying for years. It didn't lesson the pain of losing her mother, but it did free her from the burden of its secret.

As a grandchild of Survivors, I have been asked to speak publicly about what Papa's story means to me. One time was to a group of children of Survivors and they had lots of questions. Was I fearful? Did I carry guilt? They wanted to know how I had been affected, as they were afraid of passing those specific behaviors down to their own offspring. I answered that while there were certain parts of my personality that would not have otherwise been present had my grandparents not gone through the Holocaust - like why I don't waste food and why I am particularly sensitive to injustice – I'm a pretty well-adjusted person.

But on another occasion I spoke about being a grandchild of Survivors to a room full of actual Survivors. In that setting there were no questions. In fact, the tone was about hope. Looking up at me, those faces - wrinkled, hair all white - were full of appreciation. They may have been the faces of parents, grandparents and great-grandparents, of doctors or accountants or businessmen, but underneath the gold jewelry, healthy tans and fancy clothes, were people who had faced starvation and murder in an insane world. Each face was a mask shielding stories of tragedy that they themselves may not have wanted to remember, but were truly thankful I was remembering for them.

As I spoke to them, my voice shaking with emotion, my grandparents, Murray and Tosia, watching from the front, beamed with pride as I explained how I felt when I first learned about the Holocaust. How it wasn't just a lesson about my own family's history, but a lesson on human nature and the world. I talked about the responsibility I felt to tell Papa's story, to continue the dialogue, and to make sure others know what actually happened to real people.

When I finished speaking, I was hugged and kissed by Survivors thanking me for acknowledging their suffering and their survival. I realized that every one of them had their own story like Papa's.

One frail, elderly woman gripped my arm. "You're an inspiration," she said, the blue tattoo of numbers visible on her forearm. "You are why we did what we did to survive. You make it worth it."

By the time I sat down, my own eyes full of tears, my cheeks stained by several shades of lipstick, Papa covered my hand with his.

"Feigela," he said to me. "Now you see why I want you should finish the book?"

Acknowledgements

This book would not have been possible were it not for the courage and determination of one person: my grandfather, Murray Schwartzbaum. Not only did Papa Murray survive monstrous atrocities once, but he dared to do so again and again, every time we worked together on The Book.

Friends and relatives have also been of great help by their encouragement and support. I especially thank my sisters Jackie and Meredith, and my aunt Marcia Boland Wells for their honest feedback to Papa's story; my cousins Joe and Donna Sillman for encouraging me to go to Poland to see my roots; to Tsila Greenberg, Ayala Kulikovsky and Ronit Gilboa, my Israeli cousins, for their personal guided tour of Szczekociny. To my uncles Mark and Sidney Schwartzbaum for agreeing to revisit a past they had tried so hard to forget, plus a special thank you to Uncle Mark for always welcoming me into his home whenever I needed a quiet place to write.

To my grandmother Tosia for daring to confront memories of a horrible time, and for all those loving delicious meals that kept Papa and me nourished while we worked.

I especially thank my father Richard for his diligent, steady and numerous edits. Every time you asked, "Got a fresh red pen?" it made me feel good, knowing the book was only getting better.

And finally, thank you to my mother Shelly, whose endless support has no boundaries. You are a true survivor with a heart of gold and an endless capacity for love and compassion.